A

COOL

EXPERIENCE

Script by

John Sheridan Thomas

December 10, 2014

PREFACE

A COOL EXPERIENCE is about climate science. It is presented in a fictional setting, and consists of conversations among a science professor and her students probing into the consequences of carbon dioxide emissions on the earth's ecosystem.

Climate science should be a real concern to everyone. The economy of the nation and indeed the entire world is being impacted for better or worse by the manner in which we respond to fears arising from human-induced carbon dioxide emissions into the atmosphere.

We need assurance that valuable natural resources are not abandoned without appropriate and certain benefits to mankind. We cannot get that assurance unless we probe deeply and objectively into claims of global warming and its dire consequences.

Astro College
of
Science & Mathematics

CLIMATE SCIENCE 101

Participants

Professor Connie, PHD

Stu: Any student in a class of 21

LECTURES

1. CARBON DIOXIDE EMISSIONS

Prof. Connie: We burn so much fossil fuels – coal, oil, gasoline – that there is more CO_2 going into the air than can be rinsed out in a short time period.

Stu: Isn't carbon dioxide good for plant growth.

Prof. Connie: Yes it is. But carbon dioxide emissions are accelerating. Here are the last three ten-year increments of CO_2 emissions:

1990	21,000 teragrams of CO_2
2000	24,000 teragrams of CO_2
2010	32,000 teragrams of CO_2

Stu: What is a teragram?

Prof. Connie: It is an unusual unit of weight. One teragram is equal to 10^{12} grams; a rather large number of grams to be sure, but then we are talking about the entire globe.

Stu: Whatever – it's a big number!

Prof. Connie: These emissions have increased the CO_2 suspended in the earth's atmosphere. As you see in chart 1, the amount of atmospheric CO_2 increased some 25% since 1958.

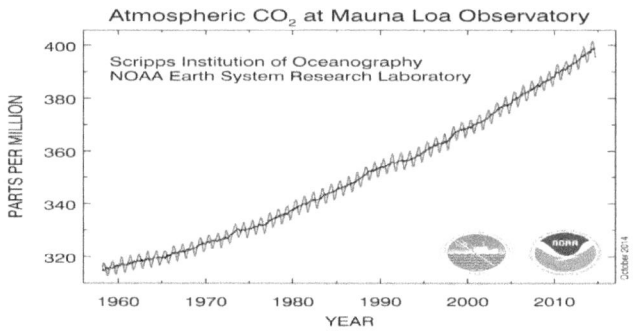

Stu: Wow! That's a huge increase. Will this cause us problems breathing?

Prof. Connie: Not at all.

Stu: So CO_2 is not bad for us and it is good for plants. How much CO_2 are we talking about anyway?

Prof. Connie: CO_2 in the atmosphere has risen to about 400 ppm.

Stu: ppm?

Prof. Connie: That's "parts per million".

Stu: Sorry, what I am wondering: what makes up the atmosphere, and what portion is CO_2?

Prof. Connie: Here are the ingredients of the atmosphere not counting water vapor.

Nitrogen	78%
Oxygen	21%
Argon	0.93%
Carbon dioxide	0.04%
Other	0.03%

Stu: Look at that carbon dioxide! That's 0.0004 parts of the total. Its' such a tiny fraction of our atmosphere!

Prof. Connie: Well . . . yes. That's correct.

Stu: Even if you doubled it, it would amount to less than one-tenth of one percent. And besides, doesn't the CO_2 in the air gradually dissipate?

Prof. Connie: Let's look closer at CO_2 behavior. Total atmospheric CO_2 is equivalent to about 1/3 of the yearly emission rate. Specifically, 6.2 ppm of CO_2 are discharged into the atmosphere each year (mainly from burning fossil fuels and cement manufacturing) while the net increase in atmospheric CO_2 is about 2 ppm.

Stu: Ah, so a large portion of the emissions are rinsed out of the atmosphere every year.

Prof. Connie: Yes 2/3. The residual CO_2 is a consequence of the rate of emission less the rate of rinsing. At some point the atmosphere likely will approach equilibrium where both rates converge and the atmospheric CO_2 stabilizes.

2. GLOBAL WARMING

Prof. Connie: Global warming is believed to be the consequence of a CO_2 greenhouse effect. Just as a greenhouse provides warmth from the sun yet prevents much of the heat from escaping, thus apparently does CO_2 prevent heat radiating outward from escaping the earth's ecosystem.

Stu: How does that work? I mean, how does CO_2 act like a greenhouse? The glass on a greenhouse is a physical barrier to prevent warm air escaping.

Prof. Connie: Likening global warming to a greenhouse is a convenient metaphor for a more complex phenomenon.

Carbon dioxide does not interfere with the light rays arriving from the sun, but it absorbs radiation arising from the earth. Hence CO_2 collects and diverts heat that otherwise would exit the planet. The reason for this, that is the short answer, is the difference in wave lengths between the sun's incoming rays and the radiation waves arising from the earth.

The CO_2 molecules absorb some of the rays rising from the earth, then as they get sated so to speak, they emit rays in all directions – some outward and some earthward.

Prof. Connie: In this way some radiation gets recycled back toward earth.

Stu: So global warming from CO_2 is real?

Prof. Connie: We know with certainty that airborne CO_2 causes some warming. What is not known is how much warming; and the range of this uncertainty is huge.

The great weakness here is the assumption that CO_2 molecules comprising just 4 of 10,000 parts of the atmosphere can divert enough heat radiation back to the earth to measurably raise temperatures globally.

Reality is we simply don't know how sensitive the earth's temperature is to additional CO_2. I believe it is far less than climate models suggest.

3. CLIMATE MODELING

Prof. Connie: Climate scientists have constructed computer models to quantify the relationships of multiple characteristics of the earth's environment; especially to predict how global temperatures are affected by airborne carbon dioxide.

These models show a direct relationship between carbon dioxide in the atmosphere and global temperatures. CO_2 increases in the atmosphere drive up the earth's temperature - according to their computer models, of course.

They include formulas shrouded in terminology that is foreign to everyone else. To fully understand them, you would need to study the physics and how the models are constructed.

Stu: If you say so. But on the other hand, they have emphatically stated that carbon dioxide causes global warming – the more carbon dioxide we put into the air, the warmer we get. There is no equivocation here, no maybes, no "well it depends on . . .". I don't need to be an expert on climate modeling to get the bottom line that more carbon equals more heat.

Prof. Connie: Quite correct; you do not. However, we have not gotten to the bottom line.

Stu: OK. So we have complex formulas that account for all of the relevant variables?

Prof. Connie: Apparently so. At least we are told that all of the relevant variables are considered. Surely the validity of modeling depends entirely on that.

Stu: But airborne carbon dioxide seems rather miniscule to me. It is hard to imagine how such great consequences can depend on such little CO_2.

So what about rising temperatures?

Prof. Connie: What about them?

Stu: Well, I heard that global temperatures stopped going up. In fact, they may be declining.

Prof. Connie: Global temperatures have been increasing for the last 100 years. The cumulative increase has been about 1 degree centigrade. Climate model projections predict the increase to accelerate through the 21st century. (Assuming we don't halt carbon emissions of course.)

Stu: But that temperature prediction is a product of their climate model. What you put in, you get out! Anyway I found this chart on the WUWT website. That's whatsupwiththat.com.

CHART 2
GLOBAL TEMPERATURE CHANGE

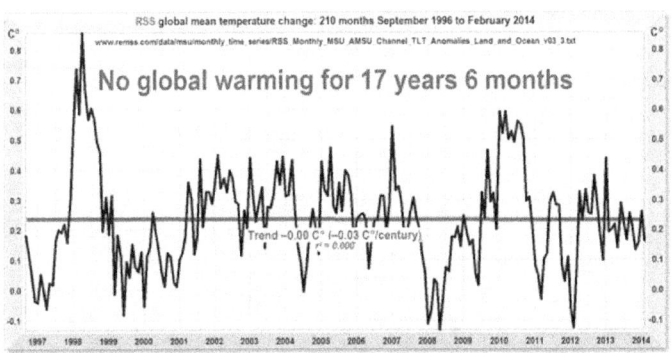

RSS global mean temperature change: 210 months September 1996 to February 2014

No global warming for 17 years 6 months

Stu: Curiously I couldn't find any global temperature data on the EPA website! Do you think they are hiding something?

Prof. Connie: Your chart shows incremental temperature changes. Temperatures are not yet declining; rather the rate of increase is now virtually zero.

Stu: Declining or flat - either way this is a long time that the models are not predicting temperature very well, especially considering their models are not much older than that.

Prof. Connie: Years of modeling experience has little to do with it. On the other hand, the carbon dioxide/global warming record indeed is quite limited. And yes, the International Panel on Climate Control is having considerable difficulty explaining this recent abnormality.

4. CLIMATE MATHEMATICS

Prof. Connie: There are several ways to conduct correlation studies. The simplest is a linear, single dependant variable study. Here's how this process works. This is an appreciation level discussion. You should get the concepts, but will not be able to conduct sophisticated analyses without help from an accomplished computer simulation modeler.

Stu: We won't be able to conduct climate analyses?

Prof. Connie: Yes, you won't. I don't think you will be able to conduct a creditable correlation analysis of any kind. Actually I am quite sure you won't.

Stu: Then what's the point?

Prof. Connie: The point is this. Understanding the principle should enable you to separate the wheat from the chaff. If not, then one of us, either you are or I am in the wrong classroom.

Stu: Boy, I sure hope it's not you!

Prof. Connie: Thank you very much. Now, here is a simple regression formula. It is hypothetical of course.

$$T = a + bC$$

Here the "T" (dependant variable) represents temperature and the "C" (independent variable) represents airborne carbon dioxide or a derivative of it, such as its logarithm.

If we had sufficient number of samples of temperature vs. carbon dioxide, the regression software could calculate values of "a" and "b" for the best fit equation. Then you could predict future temperature (T) for any amount of carbon dioxide (C) by inserting your carbon dioxide forecast into the formula and calculate the expected temperature.

This is a simple illustration. More complex models may be constructed to handle multiple independent variables and non-linear relationships.

Stu: I get the gist. You build a prediction equation; then using a lot of sample observations of T and C you calculate the coefficients needed in the equation. But why do you suggest the logarithm of carbon dioxide?

Prof. Connie: I am pleased you noticed. The logarithmic function suggests that you would have to quadruple the CO_2 to double the temperature impact, say from 1 to 2 degrees.

Prof. Connie: At 400 ppm of CO_2, the atmosphere is in a saturation region where it requires more and more CO_2 emissions to affect temperatures.

Stu: That is like . . . I got it: the Law of Diminishing Negative Returns.

Prof. Connie: I would not characterize the returns from more CO_2 as negative. Rather it increases crop yields, and in that respect at least more is better.

Prof. Connie: A caveat is in order here. You may come across a casual relationship – that is an independent variable that seems to matter, but in fact has no relevance to what you are trying to predict. If your data base is large enough, this irrelevance will become apparent. In other words, its coefficient will be nearly zero.

The larger risk is that you have not considered a variable that has real significance. In that case, sooner or later your model will fail.

Let's return to the anomaly that recent temperatures are not rising as predicted. This suggests that there are important variables not accounted for, either within the earth's sphere or perhaps in the larger solar system.

Stu: Professor, are you suggesting that the global warming science is wrong?

Prof. Connie: We are talking about modeling. One possible explanation has been offered – that the missing heat in recent years is entrapped deep in the ocean where we are unable to measure it.

Stu: Oh great! We have heat in the atmosphere warming downward; but only when it is not warming upward from the bottom of the sea!

Prof. Connie: More likely it is a symptom that the global warming science is unsettled.

There is another possibility. It is that solar activities have an unrecognized impact on global weather and temperature. NASA says there is evidence of a relationship between solar activity and global climate. They noted a long period of solar activity coincided with the lowest temperatures recorded during the "little ice age" from 1500 to 1850. Almost no sun spots were observed during that period.

Stu: Are sun spots relevant?

Prof. Connie: I believe NASA just answered that question.

Stu: Oh . . . yeah.

5. RISING SEAS

Prof. Connie: According to the National Oceanic and Atmospheric Administration (NOAA), sea level is on the rise. Using tide gauges, they measured a rise over the 20th century of 2/3 inch per decade. More recently satellite altimeter data from 1993 to 2003 shows a rise of 1.25 inch. However, it is widely believed that this rise is exaggerated: that the real rise was perhaps one-half inch more or less.

Stu: How deep is the ocean?

Prof. Connie: The average depth is about 22,000 feet. Where are you going with this?

Stu: NOAA is able to measure a change of 1.25 inches or less over 10 years – in oceans which average some 22,000 feet deep? This is in an environment of varying ocean currents, tides and depths that increase toward the equator and decline at the poles.

Prof. Connie: I assume you are referring to the centrifugal force created by the earth's rotation. Is there a question somewhere there?

Stu: Uh, no, I guess not. I'm just awed at the technology to measure such miniscule changes.

Stu: Anyway, it is hard to imagine a global crisis from a 1.25 inch increase, or even less as you suggested.

Prof. Connie: Let's look at what the experts say.

Here is an excerpt from the NOAA web site.

> As sea level rises, water inches upward along the base of vertical sea cliffs. However, even a small vertical rise can result in seawater covering huge areas of flat beaches and low-lying land. If sea level rises quickly, the encroaching ocean can drown costal marshes and disrupt seaside ecosystems. Higher seas also enable storm surges to travel farther inland, putting more lives in danger and increasing the risk to property when powerful storms come ashore. People who live on low land may have to decide whether they should raise the elevation of their homes, try to protect the land with engineering projects such as levees or seawalls, or move inland. Higher sea levels may also submerge docks in shipping ports, decrease the clearance available for ships to pass under bridges, and threaten vital sources of fresh water along coasts.

The Environmental Protection Administration says about the same thing with more emphasis on the eco systems in coastal regions.

Prof. Connie: In case we are not getting the message, EPA's climate website features a photo of a single-family suburban home submerged in four feet of water. Source of the flood water is unspecified.

Stu: Seems like EPA and NOAA are reading from the same playbook.

Prof. Connie: Yes, but the only place playbooks may be deemed science is in professional football.

Stu: Professor, where is all of this water coming from that is going to flood the world?

Prof. Connie: Supposedly it will come from melting polar ice caps, but the physics doesn't support that claim.

Stu: Really?

Prof. Connie: Unfortunately it is difficult to audit scientific pronouncements where the calculations are not revealed. My guess using published data and otherwise estimating is that the claim of world-wide flooding were the Greenland ice cap to melt is grossly exaggerated.

Stu: With all due respect ma'am, that sounds like uh . . . an unsupported critique of an unfounded claim!

Prof. Connie: I suppose so. Support, such as it is, is presented in the handout titled "Global Flood Threat". (Please refer to page 22).

Your assignment is to estimate how much the seas would rise if the Greenland ice sheet were to melt 305 feet from the top?

Stu: Why 305 feet?

Prof. Connie: Because that is the height of the Statue of Liberty.

Stu: Should we have known that?

Prof. Connie: No, but now you do. Here is the data you are to use:

> Size of Greenland = 2,166,000 km²
> The ice sheet covers 70% of the island
> Average density of the first 310 feet depth = 50%
> Total area of the world seas = 3.62 *10⁸ km²

Calculate the amount of water flowing into the oceans. Then divide that number by the total surface area of the seas. Finally convert the results into inches.

Stu: Inches? So this is not a catastrophic scenario. What's the answer?

Prof. Connie: I don't do homework. Do the math and find out for yourself.

6. BOTTOM LINE

Stu: Professor Connie, there seems to be a disconnect here.

Prof. Connie: How so?

Stu: Well, we have progressed from miniscule airborne carbon dioxide increases to the earth warming in fractions of degrees, if at all. Along the way sea-levels have risen fractions of an inch.

Everything is in tiny fractions. Then we jump to dire threats of global flooding.

Prof. Connie: As we have seen, the connections between CO_2 emissions, global warming and rising seas are tenuous at best.

Stu: Tenuous, huh! Well then, Professor Connie, what's the bottom line?

Prof. Connie: We are beset by global flooding threats and dire consequences if we continue to advance world economies by burning fossil fuels. Seas will rise as much as 26 feet. All of this is unsubstantiated.

Prof. Connie: Planet earth has been around for billions of years. It has gone through warming and cooling cycles without human interference. More important, we are a captive of the solar system. Planet earth abides by the rules of that system.

The earth is a traveler. Its angle as it sweeps around the sun produces massive weather changes. Also planet earth has a wobble which produces more weather upheavals.

The sun is a traveler too. It circles the black hole at the galaxy's core every 226 million years. Over the years it passes through tsunamis of cosmic rays which also produce massive climate changes.

Stu: Ok! We can't do anything about any of that. So, where does that leave us?

Prof. Connie: Coming down to earth, it is self-deceit to believe limited carbon dioxide in the air can destroy civilization. These are transitory molecules – they do not stay suspended in the atmosphere very long.

Stu: That's the bottom line?

Prof. Connie: Be patience please. Contrary to doomsday purveyors, the seas are our saviors. As the sun warms the earth and seas, water evaporates and rises. This leads to increased cloud density which in turn blocks the sun's radiation.

My estimate is that the potential warming from a 50% increase in airborne CO_2 would be offset by a mere 5% increase in low-level clouds.

And so, the bottom line is this. Increasing atmospheric CO_2 along with accelerating water evaporation, cloud formation and recycling back to earth mitigates global temperatures while helping to grow food for the world's population.

Stu: Wow! That's a revolutionary idea!

Prof. Connie: Actually it's basic physics.

What was "science" centuries ago is now fodder for historians. And so it will be as we stumble forward.

Stu: Let's hope we don't shoot ourselves in foot along the way.

Prof. Connie: Quite so!

END

Handout A: Global Flood Threat

The theory of global warming is that human-induced carbon dioxide emissions cause a greenhouse-like effect that prevents heat from escaping the earth's ecosystem. As the airborne CO_2 increases, global temperatures rise. Polar ice caps melt pouring massive water into the oceans; seas rise inundating major population centers of the world.

If this theory is wrong, then the threat of global flooding is moot. Even so, the consequences of public policies aimed at curtailing CO_2 emissions are real and costly, whether justified or not; so it is appropriate to inquire as to the validity of the flooding threat.

The threat is specifically linked to Greenland; and the claim is that if the Greenland ice sheet were to melt entirely the seas of the world would rise some 26 feet. Such an event would indeed be catastrophic.

Apparently the flooding threat is based on the following calculation.

A = Volume of Greenland ice sheet = 2,850,000 km^3
B = Surface of the earth's oceans = 3.62 x 10^8 km^2
C = Sea rise (A divided by B) = 7.9 meters = 26 feet

This calculation is simplistic. It ignores several basic physical considerations. They are:

The specific gravity of the ice sheet increases gradually from 15% to 80% as the depth increases. Hence upon melting the volume of ice and snow contracts immensely.

Part of the ice sheet is below sea level (the frozen inland sea). Upon melting, none of this water flows to the ocean; rather its shrinkage creates space for some above-sea-level melt.

As the seas rise, surfaces of the oceans increase, enabling more water to be absorbed for each inch of increased depth. This surface increase derives from both beach flooding and addition of a Greenland inland sea.

Each of these factors contributes to lessening sea-level rises. Collectively they are of a magnitude that invalidates the threat of massive global flooding.

On a more visceral level, we might ask why the seas have not risen more than a fraction of an inch during the 15 year period (1992 to 2007) when the Greenland permanent ice sheet surface area contracted approximately 25%.

*   *   *   *

Handout B: Suggested Readings

Dark Winter by John L. Casey, Space Shuttle Engineer and NASA Consultant.

Climate Crises in Human History by the American Philosophical Society.

Why Politicized Science Is Dangerous by Michael Crichton.

No Need to Panic About Global Warming in the Wall Street Journal, January 27, 1012, signed by 16 scientists including Antonio Zichichi, President of the World Federation of Scientists.

The Author

John S. Thomas was Deputy Director of the Budget, City of New York during the second John Lindsay mayoral term. There he directed a city-wide productivity improvement program that achieved nationwide acclaim.

Subsequently John wrote **"So, Mr. Mayor, You Want to Improve Productivity . . ."** published by the National Commission on Productivity and Work Quality in cooperation with the Ford Foundation.

He has extensive management consulting experience with major industrial corporations and the Department of Defense. He is a graduate of the University of Pennsylvania, Towne School of Engineering.

John's uncle Charles Ward Thomas commanded the United States Coast Guard icebreakers USCGC *Northland* and USCGC *Eastwind* that served in the Greenland Patrol during World War II. Admiral Thomas authored **Ice is Where You Find It.**

Contact: jthomas@oghma.us